MW01147245

The Other Love

FARRAR STRAUS GIROUX

NEW YORK

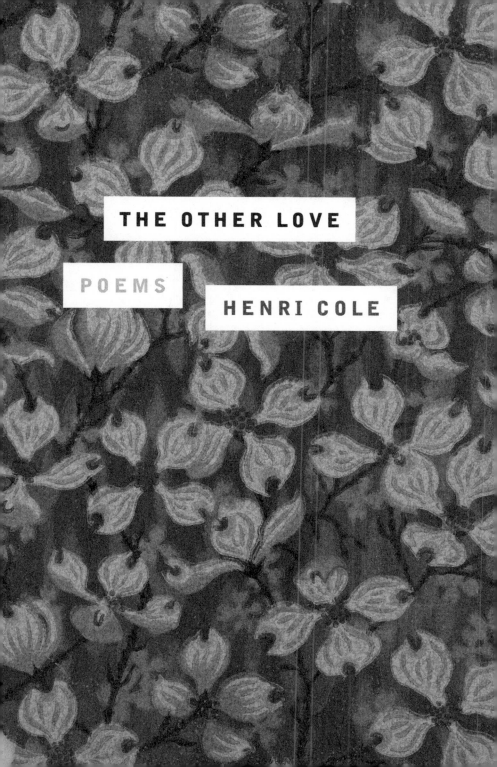

THE OTHER LOVE

POEMS

HENRI COLE

Farrar, Straus and Giroux
120 Broadway, New York 10271

EU Representative: Macmillan Publishers Ireland Ltd, 1st Floor,
The Liffey Trust Centre, 117–126 Sheriff Street Upper, Dublin 1, DO1 YC43

Art on title page and page 59: Charles E. Burchfield, *Dogwood*, circa 1923–24,
M. H. Birge & Sons wallpaper #3274, 27⅝ × 21½ inches, Gift of J. Frederic Lohman,
1992, reproduced with the permission of the Charles E. Burchfield Foundation.

Library of Congress Cataloging-in-Publication Data
Names: Cole, Henri, author.
Title: The other love : poems / Henri Cole.
Description: First edition. | New York : Farrar, Straus and Giroux, 2025.
Identifiers: LCCN 2024049208 | ISBN 9780374619039 (paperback)
Subjects: LCGFT: Poetry.
Classification: LCC PS3553.O4725 O84 2025 | DDC 811/.54—dc23/eng/20241115
LC record available at https://lccn.loc.gov/2024049208

Designed by Crisis

Our books may be purchased in bulk for specialty retail/wholesale,
literacy, corporate/premium, educational, and subscription box use.
Please contact MacmillanSpecialMarkets@macmillan.com.

www.fsgbooks.com
Follow us on social media at @fsgbooks

10 9 8 7 6 5 4 3 2 1

FOR LOUISE GLÜCK

At the terminus, unrecognizable shapes emerged—
rather than barrenness, more life.

CONTENTS

I

Friends are better than guns.

MOUSE IN THE GROCERY

There are no bacon strips this morning,
so a mouse ponders a pound of sugar.
A mouse wants what a mouse wants,
salt-cured pork instead of soluble carbs.
A mouse is like a heart: it sleeps in winter;
it knows uncertain love; it appears to have no gender.
Now this mouse regards a woman sprinkling water
on lettuce as a man pushes a broom up the aisle.
None of us knows what to expect out there.
Surely pain is to be part of it,
and the unwelcome intrusion of the past,
like violent weather that makes a grim chiaroscuro
of the air before a curtain of rainwater falls.
I clutch my basket and push on.

KOMOREBI

As I awake, iridescent light penetrates
pines in the backyard. On the television,
helicopters and armored vehicles confront young people.
Though I've lived in some faraway places,
this was not when momentous events occurred.
No one ever shouted in my face, "Damn your soul!"
I live in a house, like a mouse in a date palm.
Some nights, I dream of smoking opium,
but mine is a cautious, quiet life: my belly is supple;
I rent an upright piano; I feel sorry about Adam and Eve,
but I cannot fix things. Inside the walls of my abode,
I am a novitiate to the Art of Poetry.
Though I dig home cooking more than threesomes,
I would never say, "You are so fine, Henri."

WINTER SOLSTICE

Claire says the day will be one second longer.
Darkness will no longer exceed light.
But the weather is abysmal,
so hatred of gloom is not an option. I want to live
to be ninety-five, too, and still be assembling
words into music and truth. For now,
I regard a conference of stars, with fast-moving clouds.
Sometimes my dreams are like explosion pits,
with scary lava. Yet the Earth remains constant,
tilting away from the sun and back,
like a robin to a bare branch.
Be somebody with a body, the stars command;
Don't be a nobody. I know them by heart,
as they sink and as they rise.

TIME AND WEATHER

Now the spell is broken. A gold light traces
a line across the sky, which had been so dark,
without a cloud to be seen from one horizon
to the other. Now darker emotions dissolve.
Violence seems dumb. Things that were come back.
A red bird circles around a bush. A woman ties
the sandal of a child. A new president speaks
not of power but of our souls. Likewise,
the grass upon the mountain trembles
greener, reproducing itself while strug-
gling against human rivals. A friend asks,
"When do we leave for happiness?" Friends
are better than guns. This morning, I eat
warm corn bread with butter and jam. I walk.

GUNS

Stick-in-the-mud, old fart, what are you doing
to get the guns off the streets? I am not here to pick
on anyone. But now that they have shot Yosi,
who ground my meat in Hingham, and his shiny pink
meat truck is for sale, I feel desolate. A gun is
a vengeful machine exacting a price. A gun rejects
stillness. It wants to get off. A man can be vain—
almost like a god—but inside him is a carp biting
the muck of a lake. A man who speaks too softly
gets hit with a big stick and lopes along behind.
A gun is minatory. Still, a week of kindness is greater.
Run, hide, evacuate; don't fire, duck, take cover.
At Yosi's ceremony, his family put a gold cloth on his face.
Self-reliant, autonomous, tough, he lay in a shroud of silk.

FIGS

Overnight the figs got moldy and look like little brains—
or ids without structure—that say something dark
about our species not really laying down a garden
but living out the violent myths.
An insect chorus, almost diaphanous
in a neighbor's yard, says something, too:
America began in tall ships that glowed from within,
but for the wretched, it still wretchedeth every day.
As the bright day goes around the sun,
why do the weeks grow
more aggressive and difficult?
Why do the world's shadows
come so close
as its wonders beckon?

WHITE VIOLETS

Since a Black president took the oath of office
on Lincoln's Bible, America has been vibrating,
so I pay my taxes and adopt a respectful manner.
I haven't yet been told to get down on my knees,
but wide is the gate that leadeth unto destruction.
They were a handful of men without much money
or experience, far from the streets of their universe.
I think they probably didn't know their own strength,
going outside the everyday thoughts of our world,
and far beyond the limits of what is permitted,
but this isn't an apology, because when night falls,
they move about in confinement now,
their eyes like white violets tinged with red.
Nobody there in the palace of justice.

THREE VULTURES IN A BIRDBATH

On the back lawn that is so green this summer, with the help of chemicals from Fredericks & Son,

sitting together after a binge lunch, three vultures in a little cement birdbath,

with heads and necks tucked in, urinate straight down their legs to cool off.

They look like a committee at a wake. They do not care that nobody admires them.

They are not embarrassed by their own insignificance.

Their existence is not dependent on anyone else for its status,

certainly not the gods who created them from clay and fire, giving them the attributes they needed for survival,

so that later, when it was our turn, there were no gifts left over for us.

Now soldiers sleep in the pink granite corridors of the Capitol, soldiers who must carry around seventy pounds:

gloves, socks, glasses, phone, batteries, knife, fork, razor, toothbrush, flashlight, compass, camo cream;

soldiers, whose best friend is a rifle with detachable magazine and telescoping,

soldiers, who must turn a blind eye to themselves when they hear an order and feel enlarged by compliance;

soldiers, who—after the veneer of civilization is torn off—never forget the bodies alone in the rubble

and only want to get back to some kind of order.

SELF-PORTRAIT
WITH MARE AND FOAL

The white on the mare's back is probably
from saddle sores, but her coat is shiny
(a sign of health) and they appear well-fed.
Each animal has a refined small head.
They don't seem to miss the stallion kept apart somewhere.
They don't seem to notice the lovely branching elm
that hasn't got the blight yet.
Their hearts pick up signals their eyes miss,
and the Earth appears to shine like the sun
from all of us—tacked and brushed; not kicking
or biting—just sort of chilling
and being ourselves together,
as I sit on the paddock fence,
a positive figure in unaffected light.

DAFFODILS

Sometimes I arrive with my buds closed,
and I am mistaken for scallions,
but if you cut a half inch from my stems
and put me in water, I open up and release
yellow dust from my petal cups,
like talcum sprinkled on her shoulders
after she bathes and swallows her
third tranquilizer to erase herself,
the sedative piercing right through her
like a small bunch of flowers grasped
by a hand that connects the melancholy
to something in nature urging, *Trust me*,
as the blackbirds at dawn trust
the aurora that conquers night.

MY AMARYLLIS

Sometimes in spring, I separate myself
from others to re-create the intensity of adolescence,
though probably I am just trying to survive,
like you and all the others.
Time has stripped away so many certainties
that I don't want to forget the past.
I need a stone in my pot as a ballast,
like my amaryllis. Clutching a pillow in the night,
I see kindred shapes paddling forward,
unrecognizable figures holding out their arms,
like athletes on a field. Vain as Picasso
and mechanical as a beetle, I want to make
a thing I haven't made that says,
Look how he's evolved.

HORACE

We were driving north. A sign read,
There will be no more wilderness;
I remembered my grandfather's softness
whilst hugging him when I was a little boy.
It was as if God hadn't created us naked
or defenseless and we had all we wanted.
It was as if wilderness would never cease to be.
It was as if we needn't attend to it or die.
Unlike the rat in good Horace, I am content
with my lot. "Get out of the way," I mutter
when pain approaches. We live in such tragic times,
buffeted like stone more than flesh.
Yet each day the fulgent sun rises,
and blackbirds gather on the wire.

SOW WITH PIGLETS

Here, in a plywood shed, she keeps herself sane
licking her black piglets and kissing their eyes.
She seems so confident, with thoughts running fast.
She makes my day a little better. Each night,
during the well-pig check, her teat milk carries them
off into themselves, into the single being we adults
know as the source of our own sadness.
But here, under a dispassionate night sky,
in pig time, with blue moonlight filtering
through the cedars, I ask, Why do you leave
for happiness? Why not stay around awhile?
With muddy sneakers and thick torso,
I feel saner in this place. I paid my price
and am here for the duration.

II

Don't worry; the Art of Poetry is not the subject here.

ODE TO HEARING

It's true I speak too softly and overthink things,
but golly gee I love listening to him sing
in the shower. The universe is chaotic—
I don't need to hear this to believe it—
so I'm immensely grateful when something
that at first sounds like despair then isn't,
because its very utterance is a victory.
Like many taciturn people, I live alone.
The barn owl, the rat, the moth: they see
at night because of special rods in their eyes,
but I must have special rods in my ears,
because when he sings like that it feels as if I am
being brought into existence—and I never,
never want to leave this world I so love.

A man doesn't cease to exist because he is invisible.
He is like a lone guitar, or curly neck hairs, or false water.
Pull his arm when you go by and he forgets
it once was a fin (according to Darwin).
Another year passes, never to be lived again.
I remember being touched, but I cannot be and have been.
Since we don't know if we live beyond this life,
let's give ourselves to loving—
to eyes, hands, lips, and ears.
Do you hear those birds talking—
is there anything more ravishing?
In the world of things—so animalistic and blunt—
we are but tumbles of flesh seeking definition,
like sterile florets awaiting daybreak.

CÉLIBATAIRE

The tablecloths were white and so were most of us,
like nice people waiting for something.
I remembered when I was a boy
and doing cartwheels as Father cut the grass.
I remembered when lightning struck our house
and burned a hole through my bedroom screen.
Now my wrists are as thick as magnolia branches.
Now I am part of the scenery.
My favorite garment is a topcoat.
Weddings should be make-a-friend days,
but I felt so anxious, like a vampire in the night,
as Mother chewed on mackerel
and asked: "Are you my son, dear,
or my husband?"

NEIL

My mother never forgave my father for sleeping
with Neil. "You don't need a wife," she screamed;
"You already have one!" She sounded like a whipping woman,
but she was wounded. For years, she shut herself away
in their bedroom and slept. Once, her baking was so fine
that the silverfish in our house were morbidly obese.
To think of my parents now costs me such an effort.
My heart thumps as if I might faint or die.
I hope they are resting. They were not so strong,
pulling on each other's hair when the devil seized them—
Mother, barefoot in her nightgown; Father, in his
leather slippers and Black Watch robe—
like erect white stems blurred silvery gray by pollen.
I feel so much admiration for them.

FUNGUS DAY

Turtles are not very smart, but they are smarter
than salamanders. Cleaning their aquarium,
you scrub a little plastic palm tree with your toothbrush
and think, This must be Fungus Day. Then, more profound:
Saving face doesn't really make you safe. Sometimes
the blood assays to detect the presence of an antibody.
You lift up your eyes and hear a voice saying,
"Your life has changed." A handful of earth is sprinkled
on your head. The how, where, when, you question not,
because of a quiet strength. This is life as it is now.
Farewell to embellishments. Throw away metaphor.
Don't worry; the Art of Poetry is not the subject here,
but the self, visibly present, almost element,
traversing an edge to grapple rock.

DAY RESIDUE

"Remember, this is not *The Scarlet Letter*,
with a scrap of cloth sewn to your breast pocket,"
they said. Still, he felt like a grenade with the pin
withdrawn. He was glad his mother was dead;
she had Overbearing Mother Disease.
But why did he dream of X still? Why did he need
to know what it felt like running through
the forest with his rib cage pumping air?
A horse can never catch a deer!
Now he reads for pleasure
and gets lost in books.
Now he dwells in a garden
without a collar,
though even perfection of thought
arouses wantonness.

GLASS OF ABSINTHE AND CIGARETTE

This is a poem about a man who is dead.
Sodomy laws treated him like a second-class citizen.
There were ripple effects. With the aid of stimulants,
he spoke like a truthteller and hungered for touch.
Even when repugnant, his disinhibition seemed godlike,
and what came out of him ravished me.
Alas, tolerance builds rapidly; so many lines must be
insufflated to produce that all-is-right-with-the-world euphoria:
"Feeling good. R U there. Come right now."
To keep myself sane,
I fled, dear reader,
but I'd give my kingdom
to see myself in those
dilated black eyes again.

IT IS FORBIDDEN TO FORBID

This is what I said to the pallbearer
when he pushed me away. "Are you going to shoot me,
motherfucker, for wanting to carry him, too?
Are you the cops? Are you Stalin?
Didn't you dig that mound of black earth?
I could get a lot of publicity in the local newspaper
if I shoved you back right now.
You must think you're the Pope in Rome."
With my back seizing up, I felt like I might puke,
as if I were the No. 1 mourner, a real peacock.
Even if he was the hardest man I ever faced,
why did it taste like moist grass
to parched sheep or cattle?
Why did I only see gold grains falling?

CHAT ASSIS

Pencil thin, pregnant again,
displaying your Dracula teeth,
you watch me from the steps of the Great Mosque.
Original sin will not be settled today.
If death begins in the eyes,
it is far away.
But when are your babies due?
Will they be born in the park at night?
Will they be orphans?
You and me, we are strong,
self-sufficient types—herds of one.
Licking your coat,
with high-raised head and soft tits,
you suffer not, you nomad.

RESOLUTIONS

Stop playing catch-up
with the new generation.
Spend less money. Respond: "I love you, too."
Transcribe events without distortion.
Tell the lifeguard to teach me the flip turn.
Question not *where, when, how*. Bake bread,
put on an album, turn off the cable news.
Cherish those who choose honesty over flattery.
Ignore plate lickers, sycophants, and opportunists—
nobody there. Eat salmon, mushrooms, greens.
Don't surf the net. Don't be a herd of one,
like the cardinal blinded by
the azure window glass.
BMB—"be more better."

MY IDENTITY

All my life, reading has made me feel on the verge of something,
like a bird turning in the wind to lay itself bare
before going higher—with feet stretched out behind—
higher than the indifferent trees and noisy earth.
I'm grateful to my teachers who nurtured this experience,
education being our first need after food,
for this created calm within the mutilated bower,
where I lay—still a nascent thing—
muttering language with its two beats
speaking the music of my heart, and with three my mind.
Many experience separateness as exhaustion,
but I didn't; instead, I felt so unified and whole,
as when sunshine lights up the hut and all
the ground about it is warm and dry again.

ELF-STORAGE

(WHITE LETTERS ON A BRONX WAREHOUSE)

The paradoxes and mysteries of elf identity
are not so frightening in storage. Of course,
there are arguments—affectionate and intense—
among the elves, each one grappling with basic
questions of love and elfhood. What can *I* mean
to another elf? Which elf do I want to be with?
What kind of elf do I want to be? The pleasures
of opening up emotionally as one elf to another
do not really exist in storage. Many elves with
a deep and long-standing investment in elfhood
deteriorate. A warehouse is not a good place
for an elf of prominence. It is more a place
for the brave little elves who can accept
a vague and shapeless existence.

III

The vessel is saturated, the cloth is creased.

VETIVER

The splash of rain against my windows, as wind lifts it from the
  park,
daffodils gleaming under streetlamps, morning light so full of
  softness and sounds—
a wet cardinal, a distant ambulance—the blue hydrangea on the
  kitchen table,
everything posthumous-seeming, as I read the newspaper in my
  bathrobe,
without a fever, sweat, ache, nausea, exhaustion, cough, or
  struggle to breathe.
Later, stretching out on the kitchen floor, I see the vivid sky, with
  fluffy clouds,
like the uncut hairs around my ears that give me a less austere,
  Roman look.

"Do not think of the abyss," I say to myself.
Soon the lilacs will begin their heavy exhalations in green morning
  light,
the lawn will roll out its plush carpet,
and the late-night sky will seem deeper, as swallows fly diagonally
  into it.

Once again, we'll eat endives and ham, eggs in every style, peaches
    in red wine,
and we'll forget our confinement, as the upright robins,
six feet apart, *tuk-tuk-tuk* on the wire.

MUSHROOM SOUP

Though not everyone got sick,
everyone knew someone who was.
Our houses seemed to rest not on the ground
but on the women and caregivers
who were God's one concession to us.
They said it might start with a tickle
in the throat or feeling winded
or a little pressure on the chest,
but the timing wasn't certain.
Though the World Health Organization
recommended double-masking,
I never stopped touching my face.
I lived alone and grew a tough skin.
Now it's the smells I remember mostly,

because their loss was said to be a symptom;
if I could smell the autumn—
pine needles, acorns, and roots underfoot—
this might mean another season,
if not eternal life, with wind, creeks,
birds, and maples repeating themselves.

Now life feels calmer. My heart has fewer barriers,
though sometimes I still feel like Galileo
under house arrest. At the kitchen table,
I eat mushroom soup with salad,
munching on the soft frizz of lettuce,
like the gray rabbits in the park at dusk,
as a great white bird flies round
and round in wide circles overhead.

BROTHER ADAM BEES

(NOTRE-DAME DE PARIS)

The roof burned off and the spire fell,
but the queen remained sheltered
under the corpses of others.
In the republic of bees,
you labor in darkness inside an abode—
with cupola, columns, combs, and roof—
even as the flames go high
above your little wood house
and the wax walls inside
melt into a polished swirl.
With your tongue still working,
you're allowed only slight modifications,
even as you climb over the backs
of the dead and dying.

Then in the morning—
after gorging and sleeping
in the white smoke—you emerge and fly
around the wood monument,

so happy or angry,
while mingling in a ball that sparkles.
Later, I see you floating over
the city trees, violets, and anemones,
returning home along
the usual pollination route,
with your harvesting duties done,
and bearing bits of gold—
your love-ferment—
from a long day of flower visits.

THE CAT METAMORPHOSED INTO A MAN

A man deliriously cherished his cat;
he found him handsome and affectionate
    while meowing with a soft tone.
    He was crazier than the crazies.
    This man then—with prayers, tears,
    magic, and sorcery—
    convinced fate, one fine morning,
    to change his cat into a man,
    and on this very day
    became betrothed.
    After being so fond of the cat,
    he was now madly in love;
    never did an attractive feline
    so charm his human
    as this tom did his
    extravagant husband.
    The man caressed him, the tom stroked back;
    the man couldn't find any trace of cat.
    Carrying the metamorphosis to the limit,
    he believed him to be a man in all respects and ways,
until some mice gnawing on the bedroom mat

disturbed the pleasures of these newlyweds.

Immediately the tom leapt to his feet.

He missed his nocturnal adventures.

The mice reappear and the tom crouches like a feline,

arriving just in time,

but because of his changed form,

the mice do not fear him.

The tom never ceased to feel this urge;

such is nature's force.

It couldn't care less, after a certain age;

the vessel is saturated, the cloth is creased.

From its routines,

we may try in vain to free ourselves,

but no matter what we do,

we cannot change it.

And no pitchfork or stick

will make it reform its ways;

even armed with a whip,

you cannot master nature's will.

If you shut the door in its face,

it will come back by the window.

(A variation on the fable of Jean de La Fontaine)

HISTOIRE EXTRAORDINAIRE

Today I saw a man
stand on another man,
who had been shot,
to stanch the bleeding from a femoral artery.
Everything was motionless and red.
Love is not here, I thought,
love has gone far away.
Then there was a long descent home
(*une longue descente*)
with a story to tell
(*une histoire extraordinaire*)—
how grand and gloomy
that only a little more pain
saved him.

WILD TYPE

Mutants are not so very interesting
as wild types and other natural strains,
like penguins wearing tuxedos
and tigers with black-striped orange fur.
With my regular looks and manners,
I am no mutant made of chemicals.
Still, the world makes no sense to me,
and sometimes it's as if I am wearing
the wrong eyeglasses. Then time passes—
"Life is a stream!"; people often say this,
though it isn't really my experience.
Is it possible a need to express myself
with words is the result of my wild type?
Lately, mutants have been in the news a lot,
with the South African variant and the X-Men
(superheroes led by Professor X, a telepath).
The wild types have felt a little neglected,
though letting go of certainty has almost
freed us from seeking the regard of others,
that most lowly mode of satisfaction.
Despite the nights when the moments seem

to pass like hours (from sleeplessness),
I am always so surprised and grateful,
when morning arrives, to hear my voice
asking again, with a burst of love
in my hungry, wild-type heart,
"Darling, how would you like
your eggs cooked today?"

SLOWLY IN HASTE

Those leaf blowers sure make a lot of noise.
Since love is the way, we nuzzle in the morning,
then wake up to high-decibel screaming,
dust, and exhaust smoke. More and more, being myself
seems to oppose the nature of the world. I don't want
updated privacy statements; I don't want to accept
cookies; I don't want active-shooter drills.
Lustful, moody, shy, I want to keep revising myself,
like a protean creature, but in a smartphone-free,
non-GMO space. Perhaps something like the Quiet Car.
Not hands-free though:
I want to be adjusting the sails;
a realist trims the sails
and doesn't whine about the wind.

Don't get me wrong—my life didn't turn out as expected.
Who knows what to expect out there? After
a wandering path that led over weird abysses,
I am here at the kitchen table eating cage-free eggs.
I am a HE still. It would be okay if a horn blared to herald
a finish, like in a symphony (*slowly in haste*).

We suffer the ravages of Time & Weather, like trees holding on
to their leaves for color-change. From spring to spring,
we eat and we avoid predators. The past intrudes,
the present languishes, the future is uncertain.
I hate leaving friends when the Here is so happy and present.
So I put on the radio and drink a Coke,
but why do tanks and missiles surround the garden?
Why do the wild horses neigh?

THE OTHER LOVE

It doesn't smell here.
I can be whoever I want to be.
I can leave my dull citizen-life behind,
but have you ever walked around
looking for what was already
in your hands? Standing upright,
with arms down, staring straight ahead,
I could be a statue or a pine tree.
The love-canceling hours are gone now.
There is no ick factor.
I do not cut down more than I can sow.
It's like living a simple life
in a forest, or splitting off
a part of me to grow.

You probably think that I am
more like a swan than a panther,
since tears, those most ludicrous of things,
once stuck my eyes together. But all that
is behind me now. Don't get me wrong:
sometimes I still become so excited that

my love can scarcely express itself.
Sometimes I eat a toad to prove a point.
Sometimes I succumb to flattery.
Sometimes I watch smut. But inside me,
a strange new work is underway:
I see the first stars in the Southern Hemisphere.
I imitate the gull's cry when I stand by the sea.
I love the things I love and nothing more.

AT SIXTY-FIVE

It was all so different than he expected.
For years he'd been agnostic; now he meditated.
For years he'd dreamed of being an artist living abroad;
now he reread Baudelaire, Emerson, Bishop.
He'd never considered marriage . . .
Still, a force through the green fuse *did* drive.
Yes, he wore his pants looser.
No, he didn't do crosswords in bed.
No, he didn't file for Medicare.
Yes, he danced alone in the bathroom mirror,
since younger men expected generosity.
Long ago, his thesis had been described as promising,
"with psychological heat and the consuming
will of nature." Now he thought, *This*, then, is all.

On the rooftop, in pale flickering moonlight,
he pondered the annihilated Earth.
At the pond, half a mile across was not
too far to swim because he seemed to be going
toward something. Yes, the love impulse
had frequently revealed itself in terms of conflict;

but this was an old sound, an austere element.
Yes, he'd been no angel and so what . . .
Yes, tiny moths emerged from the hall closet.
Yes, the odor of kombucha made him sick.

Yes, he lay for hours pondering the treetops,
the matriarchal clouds, the moon.
Though his spleen collected melancholy trophies,
his imagination was not impeded.

(After Hans Magnus Enzensberger)

LAMENT FOR THE MAKER

(BELLAGHY, COUNTY DERRY, NORTHERN IRELAND)

At the museum of his life,
his leather duffle coat is behind glass.
It felt like a poem-protection center.
And it was my responsibility to go home,
put food out in the same place every day,
talk to the people who came to eat,
then organize them, food and poetry being
nourishment that shares a syntax.
There were many back roads to this far town,
but at the end of a path over pluff mud
I lay my shield down and stretched out on a bank.
Woolgatherer, daydreamer, bird-dogger,
I was really sorry to have to leave,
but my hands felt less tied.

Like herons in a grove—or rain on mountains
or in a deep ravine—the realm of the immortals
releases and renews us. We want to live as if
we are going to die tomorrow. We want to learn as if

we are going to live forever. We want our bodies
to belong to us. Wider seems the path. On the train,
there was maple viewing and word games: alone, atone,
bemoan, daemon: "Thy word is all, if we could spell."
The sun seemed hush-hush, then later,
like a sword sinking through stone. At the hotel,
there was black tea and murmuring.
After supper and a bath, I felt so glad,
drinking water at the sink,
though usually I despair.

107 WATER STREET

All the sailboats in the harbor
face north. I can see twenty-four
from your study window.
Overhead, large white birds fly around
in the September glow.

The sky is baby blue without a single cloud.
The house at 25 Main Street finally sold.
Isn't that where Venture Smith lived?
He was the son of a prince, who purchased
his freedom. History cannot be unlived.

Chez Perenyi, I visited David's ashes
under a chestnut where edible mushrooms,
Phallus ravenelii, now grow, and Libby,
a rescue dog from Tennessee,
nuzzled me and licked my lashes.

At the farmers market, the cheesemonger
couldn't stop talking. A young man at Nana's bakery
gave me a brioche and smiled kindly.
And Mrs. Purity, of Purity Farm (I love her peaches),
stepped right out of a small Dutch painting.

All night, I hear the clinking halyard lines.
Before dawn, I buy a coffee at Tom's Newsstand,
then sit with your big *Petit Larousse*, La Fontaine,
and my ardor. September is a time to feel the light,
write, scratch out, write, nap, walk, begin again.

I am too afraid of jellyfish to swim
with Jonathan out to the breakwater;
instead, I sit with Penny at her long
dining table and eat beef bourguignon.
You make me feel I almost belong.

AUTUMN FERN

I hope you won't mind a fern on your grave.
Standing on the shovel to dig a deep hole,
I'm a year younger than you are now.
I've written a will and reread the old masters.
Swimming out to the breakwater, maybe
a part of me is you touching buoy 328
before turning back to the borough beach.
Maybe my hairy body is like a bee's:
eating pollen grains from a thousand flowers,
spreading nectar across the comb in darkness,
then flapping my wings to dry up the water
and hasten the creation of viscous honey.
If the lane to the dead is generative, as you said,
let this hole be a point of light.

J.I.M. (1926–1995)

YOUNG TOM'S ROOM

(GLOUCESTER, MASSACHUSETTS)

I

I'm sorry you were not my favorite.

Probably your dark substratum was too much for me.

I don't believe in Hell; therefore, I don't fear it.

I'm no possum playing dead to conceal myself.

Reading in your boyhood room, I feel like a counterpart to
    nature and the animals,

and I still prefer Marianne Moore, who created a marvelous new
    idiom.

But I love bicycling along your gray granite shoreline, from the
    boatyards to the port.

And I love watching the pea fog vanish off the icy water.

Certainly, I fear death by water more than Hell.

Yesterday, a fingerless man was selling cod.

A child peered into a rock pool at a sea anemone.

The fir trees looked thirsty and seagulls screamed in the air.

A schooner with a mermaid bowsprit sailed toward open sea.

I was wearing my trousers with the cuffs rolled up like a
    knockabout sailor.

Churchgoers emerged into the marine light, but I felt no ancestor
   worship.
Home and Mother were far away.
Still, the blue sea and birdsong beckoned to a place deep inside
   me.

II

At night, the wind howls and black waves smash against the
   rocky coastline.
There are visitations:
a skunk in the corridor, pictures awry on walls, wet pillows,
   coyotes baying.
I read all night and drink wine with pistachios.
I love the bare-rock outcroppings from glaciation that surround
   the house like staunch, comforting arms.
Tom, I agree that genuineness (your word) is more important
   than greatness.
Tom, I agree that our duty is to serve, extend, and improve the
   language.
Tom, I agree that forms have to be broken to be remade.
I don't want to write only from my head and cling to youthful
   experiences.
I don't want to become a dignified man who says what is
   expected of him.
I don't want to lose myself in a larger context, like a bee in the
   foxglove.

Clambering over rock, I study the pool's frail seaweed and the
    hungry starfish.
I hear the song of the fishermen's dories lowered into the deadly sea.
At dawn, the pure sweetness of the hermit thrush calls to me.
For all I know, the rest of my life is taking flight.

ACKNOWLEDGMENTS

For their encouragement, I am indebted to the editors of the following publications, where many of the poems in this collection, sometimes in different form, were originally published.

The Atlantic: "My Amaryllis"

The Best American Poetry: "At Sixty-Five"

Disaster Diary (artist book with Susan Unterberg and Jeanne Silverthorne): "Time and Weather"

Lana Turner: A Journal of Poetry and Opinion: "*Célibataire*" and "It Is Forbidden to Forbid"

Liberties: A Journal of Culture and Politics: "Glass of Absinthe and Cigarette," "Guns," "Horace," "Lament for the Maker," "My Identity," "'No One over Fifty, Please,'" "Slowly in Haste," "Wild Type," and "Young Tom's Room"

The New Criterion: "*Chat Assis*"

The New Republic: "ELF-STORAGE" and "Resolutions"

The New York Review of Books: "Mouse in the Grocery"

The New Yorker: "Autumn Fern,"
"Daffodils," "Figs," and "Winter Solstice"

The Paris Review: "The Other Love"

Poem-a-Day: "At Sixty-Five"

Poetry: "107 Water Street"

Radcliffe Magazine: "Vetiver"

The Threepenny Review: "Sow with Piglets"

Times Literary Supplement: "Neil"

I wish to record my thanks to the T. S. Eliot House and the James Merrill
House for hospitality and solitude during invaluable residencies.